# of War and other things

NICHOLAS RODRIGUES

This edition first published in paperback by
Michael Terence Publishing in 2022
www.mtp.agency

ISBN 9781800944084

Cover image
Nicholas Rodrigues

Michael Terence
Publishing

Contents

When

When the world is like a fire,
Burning you to the bone,
When you shout, scream, plead for help,
When you're left on your own.
When nobody cares what happens,
    or if you live or die,
Remember to keep fighting,
Fighting with all your life.

When you think that it is over,
The battle has been lost,
When you feel like a loser,
You can't win at any cost.
When your faith is drying up,
And your hope is growing cold,
Remember to keep fighting,
Remember to stay bold.

Soon there will be victory,
You'll feel gloomy no more,
Soon there will be happiness,
You'll need nothing more.
Soon you'll be at peace,
Soon you won't feel hate,
Soon you will feel different,
It is never too late.

So keep on fighting.

The Marching Men

I sat upon a rocky hill,
And watched as men marched by,
There was no glory in their step,
No inflated sense of pride.

As I watched, a friend walked past,
One I knew before the war,
Gone were his humour, his smiling face,
The shine in his eyes no more.

As he marched he noticed me,
A face that he once knew,
But on he marched with teared-up eyes,
Knowing that his life was through.

And on they marched towards the sun,
As I stood upon that hill,
I knew that soon my time would come,
To kill or to be killed.

Bloodied Snow

I stand, perplexed, in a field of snow,
My eyes glance towards the trees,
The muzzle flash, the eerie glow,
Through the bitter winter breeze.

Suddenly, the gunshots crack,
Soldiers fall all around,
The cries of officers ring 'fall back',
As all my comrades hit the ground.

The soldiers boldly stand their ground,
While the officers run,
We don't want to die,
At the hands of their guns.

They swoop in from all sides,
We find ourselves caught,
And soon we realise,
Soldiers always get naught.

The Bombs of the War

Bombs were dropping from the sky,
And tanks roving had begun,
Planes were soaring over the clouds,
Flying into the sun.

We remember the time when the war began,
And the time it ended as well,
For now we hope for a better world,
And remember when bombs still fell.

The Stain of War

The sky of which was a beautiful blue,
Is now black from where the aeroplanes flew,
For when the tanks went roving on,
They wouldn't stop till the war was won,
Though why they started they had no clue.

The men who had such peaceful lives,
Will now never see their children and wives,
Now the families have mourned all day,
Since the men were sent away,
And the glint of hope dies.

Death

The men came traveling from far and wide,
While death laughed and life cried,
For as the planes flew and the tanks drove,
And all the trucks started to rove,
The people mourned for the men who died.

The war was spreading across the world,
While hate went to souls and unfurled,
We hope now for the war to end,
And the wounds we caused to start to mend,
And hate to go to the underworld.

The Enemy

We ran across the battle fields,
Guns in our hands,
Firing and killing forever-more,
Sprinting through marshy lands.

We hid all night in trenches,
We killed all day in the sun,
We lost all the men in our army,
Every single one.

When the war was over,
We celebrated the end,
We joined together and laughed all night,
Now the enemy, is our friend.

The Gravestones of War

The poppies blew in Flanders Field,
The bodies of men underground,
Hopes and dreams shot and killed,
Buried below an earth mound.

Millions of gravestones in the earth,
Dead men below,
As a cold wind passes through the night,
Littering the ground with snow.

The Trenches

We sprinted across the marshy land,
Guns slung over our shoulders,
Enemy guns firing hard,
Smashing rocks and boulders.

We jumped into the swampy trenches,
Treading on broken glass,
Hiding from enemy soldiers,
Wishing time would pass.

Running back, the victory won,
Celebrating the end of the war,
Everyone parading round the streets,
No more death, fighting or gore.

Leaving for The War

The soldiers marched, guns in hands,
Towards the fighting and no-man's land,
They left their wives and children behind,
Not knowing what they'd find.

The families were sad, little hope in their heart,
No more of the happiness that once had part,
They couldn't stop thinking
    of the loved ones who'd left,
The ones who went to fight so deft.

Some of the men came back at the end,
The holes in their hearts starting to mend,
But some of them never came home,
Leaving their family sad and alone.

This Is
The Great War

The planes and bombs filled the sky,
As dying men gave a piercing cry,
The shells dropped from way up high,
This is the great war.

We shot and died the whole night through,
As the wind blew and blew,
This day is shared with me and you,
This is the great war.

Four years later it was the end,
As we celebrated round every bend,
We all joined as every brother and friend,
This was the great war.

The Beach of The War

The wind blew across the sandy beaches,
Or at least so they say,
A cold dark wind is blowing,
Stirring the glistening bay.

Boats sailed across the waters,
Sails raised high,
Though it was just one hundred years ago,
that men were sent to die.

It was on this very beach,
That bombs were dropped down high,
And all those young soldiers,
Let out their death cry.

Now it is all over,
And everyone's at rest,
We can all relax in comfort,
For we all know it's for the best.

Horses of War

We galloped across the field of war,
And charged towards the guns,
The enemy shot our legs and heads,
And helped their fellow Huns.

We travelled distances far and wide,
While men rode on our backs,
We drank water from metal pots,
While we followed the German's tracks.

War is A Terrible Thing

The war was coming to England,
And the men were leaving home,
They got into the tanks and trucks,
And left their families lone.

The bombs were falling down,
And the planes were firing away,
The men were shooting the Germans,
And the ships were leaving the bay.

Families In The War

We mourn all day for the ones we lost,
And protect ourselves at night,
The bombs fall and explode on the ground,
And almost kill us from fright.

We think of when the war will end,
And all is fair once more,
But now we have to help our friends,
And stop this dreadful war.

There Was A Storm

There was a storm last night,
The wind was howling loud,
Water gushed in torrents of rain,
The sky was filled with clouds.

There was a storm last night,
The hail and sleet came down,
Leaves and branches blew round the house,
Snow covered the town.

There was a storm last night,
But now it is over and done,
The rain, wind, hail and snow,
Is now forgotten and gone.

The Seasons

Snow falling,
Frosty airs,
Ice forming round
mountain hares.

Trees sprouting,
Leaves growing,
Animals scuttling,
Branches blowing.

Blossoms blooming,
Foxes feeding,
Flowers forming,
Gardeners weeding.

People harvesting,
Flowers dying,
Squirrels collecting,
Merchants buying.

The Executioner

He trudged through the sand,
An axe in his hand,
The jeers of the crowd,
A blood red cloud.

The cry of pain,
Will drive you insane,
The blood on the street
washed away by sleet.

The sun on the blade,
Another star is made,
As someone else is laid
in their hard-stone grave.

When I was A Child

I remember the times when I was a child,
Running in meadows of green,
I remember the times when I was so young,
The times when I was so keen.

I remember the times when I roamed the streets,
Living without a worry in the world,
I remember the times when I did what I pleased,
My life barely unfurled.

But now I am thin and my bones are old,
And I cannot run across the shore,
But I feel I would give anything,
To live that life once more.

Pollution

The plastics are floating upon the sea,
And the bottles are on the shore,
The birds are pecking at the bags,
And the packets are on the floor.

So please stop littering your rubbish,
Please throw it in the bin,
Help save our planet,
And don't let pollution win.

Flowers

They smell of honey and perfume,
Their dresses of many colours,
The children pick them to put in their hair,
And bring them to their mothers.

The bees start to pollinate,
And the flowers turn grey,
It allows its seeds to go loose,
And lets them go astray.

The Shadow

He stalks the day through meadows of green,
And disappears at night,
He can swim the deepest ocean,
And soar the air in flight.

He is the largest thing on earth,
But can be smallest at will,
He hunts for creatures great and small,
Though he can not kill.

When sunset comes, he's silent,
His body grows long and thin,
He shrinks away to the distance,
And darkness comes from within.

Sharks

He swims through the depths of the
dark blue waters,
The ultimate predator of the seas,
He stalks his prey all day long,
Until victory he will seize.

The fishermen come to catch the sharks,
And put them in a shop,
So help save sharks from being eaten,
And make this madness stop.

The Forest of Life

Trees that once stood proud and tall,
Were soon falling down,
The roots that had grown so strong and thick,
Have now gone shrivelled and brown.

The wood was taken away to be burnt,
Or turned into tables and chairs,
So help stop the people chopping down trees,
And don't let the victory be theirs.

Pigs

They roll around in mud all day,
Bathing in the sun,
They never want to take a wash,
Every day having fun.

They are taken to animal shows,
And kept in a pig pen,
When they grow old they are taken,
Never to be seen again.

Trees

They are green with moss from long-ago,
And leaves on the end of their sticks,
Their trunks are darkened with age over years,
The birds making chirps and clicks.

The vines are crawling up the trees,
and the birds are sitting high,
the leaves are waving in the breeze,
And the branches are reaching to the sky.

Space

It is filled with stars from long ago,
Where it ends nobody knows,
It goes on for millions of miles,
Making a bright fiery show.

It has been there for millenniums,
And longer than that it will endure,
It will stay the same forever,
And bright minds it will lure.

Books

They hold stories and fairy tales,
Written by authors abroad,
They help to fall asleep at night,
Written in classes on a board.

They bring people together,
And keep them from coming apart,
So try reading more books in the day,
And keep reading from your heart.

Smoke

It floats up from the fire's heart,
And rises up to the sky,
It burns our eyes and chokes our lungs,
And makes us want to cry.

The fire is put out by the rain,
And the smoke becomes thin,
It twists and curls towards the sky,
And disappears in a spin.

The Hunter

He shoots animals for their skin at day,
And lurks the forest at night,
He kills the birds and beasts alike,
And if he has to, he will fight,

Stop killing the animals,
Like insects and beasts and birds,
Help the animals not become extinct,
And please listen to these words.

Birds

They fly across the sky and land,
And make their nests in trees,
They cheep and chirp without an end,
And travel over the seas.

They have their little baby birds,
And feed them up with worms,
They teach them how to soar and fly,
And so the little bird learns.

The Painter

The brush swoops from side to side,
A blur of colourful light,
The canvas fills with reds, greens, blues,
A truly spectacular sight.

The easel creaks, the paintbrush moves,
Art with creative mind,
A picture is formed, a heart is warmed,
The corner of the piece is signed.

Paint is mixed, colours are made,
The picture is almost done,
Soon it will be sold away,
A new life has begun.

Many people stare and point,
A sea of amazed faces,
The painting hangs there in the room,
Watching as the crowd races.

Whales

They swim through the sea all day,
And eat plankton and fish,
They travel for millions of miles,
Though safety is a silly wish.

The whalers come to kill them,
And take their blubber and oil,
They chop them into pieces,
And cook them in tin foil.

Cats

They go to sleep during the day,
And come awake at night,
They prowl the streets and search for mice,
Their fur orange and white.

They hear every movement,
And see every bird,
They can climb up trees and jump the fences,
So fast that they seem blurred.

The Cowboy

He rode on in the dusky morn,
His cape flowing behind,
The gold and jewels from kings and queens,
In a bag with a lace bind.

He canters up to the bullring,
And scares the animals away,
He rounds them up with his pony,
And keeps them from going astray.

The Mountain Illness

And as the illness spread across the land,
It came across a gallant band.
They searched and searched for the profound cure,
But all they found was cows' manure.

Then one day at a time of bliss,
They came across a mountain, cloaked in mist.
"Let's climb that mountain." One of them said,
And so, they started straight ahead.

They climbed and climbed, and up they went,
Until they reached an old man's tent.
The old man said "travel yonder on,
'til you reach the retired don."

So, they travelled yonder on,
'til they reached the retired don.
They were told "climb higher 'til you see,
The sacred cure of the honey bee."

And so they travelled up the mountain,
'til they reached an abandoned fountain.
Atop the fountain was a statue of a bee,
They drank its water's, and were cured finally.

The Trash Monster

The litter goes in the bin,
Never thought of again,
That empty can, that bag of food,
Their destinations all the same.

Every week the monster comes,
The one that takes the trash,
It crushes the bags in its metal jaws,
Turned into a cube of mash.

On to the hill of rot it goes,
Putrid with a scent of decay,
It vomits up those rancid cubes,
And prepares for the next day.

And so there sits those empty cans,
The bags of wasted food,
They'll sit there for centuries to come,
All because of the choices you choose.

Available worldwide from Amazon

Michael Terence Publishing

www.mtp.agency

www.facebook.com/mtp.agency

@mtp_agency

Printed in Great Britain
by Amazon

87184011R00047